The Shaking City

For John

The Shaking City

Cath Drake

Seren is the book imprint of
Poetry Wales Press Ltd.
57 Nolton Street, Bridgend, Wales, CF31 3AE
www.serenbooks.com
facebook.com/SerenBooks
twitter@SerenBooks

The right of Cath Drake to be identified as
the author of this work has been asserted in accordance
with the Copyright, Designs and Patents Act, 1988.

ISBN: 978-1-78172-575-7
ebook: 978-1-78172-576-4

A CIP record for this title is available from the British Library.

The publisher acknowledges the financial assistance of the Books Council of Wales.

Cover artwork: Sadie Tierney, *Las Vegas NY NY*,
www.sadietierney.co.uk

Author photograph: David X Green.

Printed in Bembo by Severn, Gloucester.

Contents

1

The Shaking City

Sleeping in a Shaking City

I'll tell you how there is one chair then another
    and that's called sitting together.

I'll tell you about small things hidden under beds
    or in yoghurt containers dug into gardens.

About a stray cat who tiptoes across the back fence
    and through the tiny bathroom window.

I'll tell you how thin I feel; how the rain falls and falls
    but still the charcoal stains won't wash off.

Do you remember summers when cricket matches lasted
    forever and seagulls tacker-tacked on the roof?

Or watching ants for hours, imagining the risk of falling
    if each stair was so enormous?

How does a city gather its skirts before the dip of night?
    Its powerdrills and refrigeration whirring –

there must be somewhere in this town that doesn't shudder,
    somewhere I can properly sleep.

Furniture

As he reads the chapter on how he suddenly left with no explanation,
when I was wobbly and my heart had cracks that took years to heal,

alone in a foreign country, and how I couldn't make sense of it
in the skin I had on so I unpeeled and sat raw in the sun waiting

for skin to grow again, he falters, flashes red, stands up, says
he can't go on. It has pierced him in a way it didn't in the past.

I tell him not to worry, the past no longer drags at my heels.
He sits and reads again, his body swelling with it, but this time

when he stops, he's quiet in a very different way as a heavy shelf
appears hovering in the air, and as he keeps reading, every time

he pauses, a new shelf appears, then a whole bookshelf, a desk,
a table, two chairs, until the room we stood in, the room he left,

is all there: chairs never sat on, mattress bare, shelves empty,
surfaces gleaming with streaks of sunlight. The indifferent furniture

is as solid as the bodies we must live within, inside my room,
our room, in a tower block of a city that is shaking.

Why I Feel Queasy Scanning Rental Listings

It isn't my fault. It's the ground. I never bother
getting furniture to fit. Nothing just fits: things
don't find their proper place. Clothes, papers, shoes,
mugs, knickers, earrings get shoved from one day
to another. The giddiness, the seasickness is expected
and I lose things: cardigans, crockery, books. I lie in bed,
waiting for the floor to stop sliding away or pulling
in opposite directions between the lamp and couch.
It affects my sense of conviction, my resilience, my
relationships: men who stay over seem to shift oddly
by morning. There have been times when I watch
my hand rest on another's, then see it drift away when
I was sure I was sitting still. I tell myself I'll move to
somewhere stable soon, but I don't *pick* these flats –
like someone who always complains of finding lovers
the same as their absent or violent father, I'm always
hopeful but keep finding flats where the floors move.
There was Wasley Street that had such an awful
twitching slant: I'd wake up shuffled into a corner.
There were three blissful months in a big-windowed flat
on the hill of Edward Street before it started, slow at first
but before long I was standing at the bathroom basin,
my face wet, watching my bedroom inch away until
it was almost at the back fence. I waited in my socks,
sitting on the edge of the bath, feeling sad. Sometimes
I dream of a simple life where I choose what to wear
from clothes that hang in the same place every day,
matching jewellery, a silk scarf perhaps, shined brogues
and dress in an uncanny stillness, then slowly eat granola
with strawberries like those pictures on cereal boxes.

The Conferrer of Honourable Badges

There's a teacup with eyes, a clothesline sailing the high seas,
a chimney carried off by an eagle, a one-way street sign on a scallop shell,
a shield of dandelions. Fabric badges with metallic or fluorescent stitching
cover his 'office' window, a garage conversion – you can't miss it –

there's no explanation, no website. You have to *ask*. But if you
help out at the community centre, work for the council or a local shop,
he'll know about you. The office door is ajar when he's in consultation
and passers-by often loiter, pretending they're not listening.

I heard a CEO cry when he was told 'not quite' and a punk rocker
sing to the end of the street, badge held high. There are no criteria:
he awards according to 'a quality of dedication, a growth of spirit
you can't really define, very *individual*, situation-dependent'.

The Returning Money Badge isn't always bestowed when money
has been returned. The Hosting Strangers Badge is more nuanced
than the act of invitation. The Rescue Badge can apparently include
just yourself. The Travelling Alone Badge sounds straightforward

but it's an enigma as no one has been awarded it yet, despite
a burgeoning interest in pilgrimages. Strangers approach each other:
How did you get that one? and share more about their life than they expect.
Badges are sewn on jackets and backpacks, framed in hallways.

One high achiever has made a hat out of them, another a flag.
We're proud that they mark something otherwise unrecognised,
the reasons not entirely clear and it's a relief that life for all us
is often a series of mysterious chances. It helps us carry on regardless.

Truly, Deeply

Of course, he's not what he used to be,
this rickety old thing whose ribs, legs, tail,
neck and even some organs are replaced

by mechanics. The angles are never quite
the same: his hind legs jut from a wasted body
held up by his four-legged walker. I'm not sure

which parts of him are still dog. The way
he sneezes or itches isn't very dog any more.
But I don't mind because at 52 – older than me –

I'm so grateful he's alive. When he sees me,
he still has that unmistakeable dog excitement,
though faint, in the white bloom of his eyes

and jiggle of limbs, his joints rattling.
It's mostly by smell he knows me now;
I'm a fog of memory to him. His grey tongue

shakes oddly. An amber liquid drips
from the side of his mouth and the juncture
of a thigh: saliva, plasma, lubricating oil

or a mixture of body and machine.
A heady infusion masks his raw scent
and the waft of musky fuchsia odoriser

is like nothing I've ever known. Oh yes,
his bike basket, canoe-companion,
pulling-roller-skates heyday is long gone.

I wouldn't handle a stick or speak
the word 'cat' for fear he'd injure himself
or worse. I sit upright in bed listening

for his squeaky limbs. I know it's him:
my first love, my childhood dog.
Now he's become mostly a feeling.

What I'm Making With the World

I'm making a handbag out of the hide of the world.
I'd been hunting for something contemporary, unique.
It gutted and skinned fairly easily: the soil, rivers, oceans,
seams of hot tar, broken glacier chips and molten yolk
fell out into a pile that I'll take in a sack to the tip.

I'd rather not bury it in the yard for the dog to dig up
and there are some nuclear power stations, chemical dumps,
explosives, cracked pipelines that could cause complications.
Recycling won't work so I'd rather get rid of the lot,
drive it there in the ute and stop off for craft supplies.

I've cured the hide so the pretty mountains, valleys and cities
won't lose their colour. I artfully cut around the best bits:
the Alps, Machu Picchu, Pyramids, Petra and ditched
the ugly stuff: Calcutta, Guatemala, Brisbane, Houston,
endless boring tower blocks and deserts, bland wheatfields.

My secret is a custom diamond needle – the hide was tough
in places. I had to stitch through Paris to make a pocket
and a charming button obscures half the Himalayas
but it's very stylish and when I take it to the gala dinner
I'm sure there'll be admiring looks, jealousy most likely.

How I Hold the World in This Climate Emergency

Sometimes I hold world in one hand, my life
in the other and I get cricks in my neck
as the balance keeps swinging. I walk uneasily.

Sometimes I am bent over with the sheer weight of world,
eyes downcast, picking up useful things from the ground.

Sometimes one shoulder is pulling toward an ear
as if it's trying to block the ear from hearing but can't reach.

Sometimes my body is a crash mat for world. I want to say
'I'm sorry I'm sorry!' but don't say it aloud.
I am privileged so I should be able to do something.

Sometimes I lie on my side and grasp world like a cushion.
I'm soft and young, and don't feel I can change anything.
I nudge world with affection, whispering: I know, I know.

Sometimes I build a cubby from blankets thrown across furniture.
There is only inside, no outside. When I was a child,
world was a small dome and change came summer by summer.

Sometimes I make a simple frame with my arms to look at world.
I'm not involved directly. It carries on without me.
This way I can still love the sky, its patterns of clouds and contrails.

Sometimes I'm chasing world through the woods, bursting
with hope and adrenalin. Oh God, am I running!
I want to keep moving. My mouth is full of fire.

Some days are like bread and milk. I just get on with pouring
and buttering. I want the little things to be what matters most again.

Sometimes I hold little: I'm limp and ill.
Days barely exist. It's enough to make soup.

Dhanakosa, Scotland

The mist came through the glen, past the waterfall
       roaring vertical, sweeping through trees,
the sturdy quivering stems of wildflowers and vines,
       and uncurled itself across the loch.
A heron appeared from the grass, craned its neck,
       lifted its legs and steered its insect-like body
to pierce the mist, disappearing into it
       with flashes of grey-white, grey-white.

There was a track through a gate: *To McLaren Craig* –
       uphill, downhill, where heather and bluebells
lined the path to a forest floor crowded with planets of moss
       and mushrooms scattered like pebbles.
Then a sudden drop and an almost 360-degree view
       of raw mountains, glens, a toy town below
with stone houses, a cemetery and cobbled streets. The mist
       rested coyly in puffs in the valleys and hillsides.

Two lovers appeared at the lookout and came close
       to the edge. She had a mouth like milk;
he had no shirt on. The mist hung just above the earth
       with the illusion of being held, the hope
of a soft landing. Then it sprawled across the armchair
       of the hilltops, lolling in mountain air and the sky
splayed clouds like a suspended ocean. The blue-black loch
       flickered its startled eyes in the sun.

As the late afternoon glowed through the lace of trees,
       the rocky edges became softer, cooler.
The mist was hovering above and the loch was so glassy
       it held the veins of valleys, hillsides, sculpted trees
and the arc of sky in minute detail –
       it made the impossible seem possible, opposites visible.
The mist exhaled a burst of tingling wind and the valleys
       shuddered then readjusted themselves.

Past waterlilies shivering in their reflections, the stream
        rushing to be with them, a boulder where heather
climbed to the top sending blossoms skyward,
        was the biggest mountain outlined in electric orange
and a wash of mist infused into the loch in alternately still
        and rippled onyx sheaths. The mountains, trees,
glens, sky were a cave around me; the blue-winged dragonfly
        dived and tapped my knee on its way past.

The Flowers of Our City

Here flowers are airborne: their petals
catch on a twig or window sill, their roots
shoot toward the sky, seeking air,

more air, the flow of wind, tides, breath,
the waft of steam from an air conditioner.
They billow over the city as we talk.

Daisy, geranium, boronia, hibbertia,
mess up our hair, stroke our foreheads.
At times we want our feet to fly up too,

our hands to reach for the ground, while
tickets, tissues, coins fall out of pockets.
We want to be blossom, immerse in scent.

An astonishing blue lechenaultia hooks
around a street lamp. A grevillea tendril
flits inside an open notebook. There's comfort

in fine gold hibiscus pollen appearing
on an outstretched hand and purple hovea
curling inside a window, trembling.

We marvel at gravity and the pull of sun.
A poppy and its bee can dangle toward me
just when I need to be drawn back to the earth

from despair. Here, all feels as it should.
Our windpipes and delicate neck muscles
quiver with gerberas, isopogons, myrtles.

Shaky School Album

1. Corner Block Vigil in Cowboy Hat

I'm five years old, crouched on the knee-high brick fence
next to the letter box. I've scraped my legs getting up there.
I'm wearing a cowboy hat and a man's striped dressing gown
with long red beads, and watching cars choose their direction.
My fists are clenched as if I'm clutching an imaginary railing.
The deep green well-cut lawn all around me is a sea for pirates.
Rose bushes that run along the path to the house are stubborn islands:
they bloom outrageously or are cut back to swords of thorns.
Perhaps I'm waiting to be lifted off, life to hoist its skirts,
the street to rouse or the shaking inside me to rattle open until tins
screwed tight in cupboards of cupboards back in the house burst.
I'm waiting for years to roll out: school term after term pulling
each other along, me trailing in a wonky wheelbarrow, beads jangling.

2. Show-off with Superior Scotch

So arrogant. *I know this, and that. And that.*
He came from a dynasty of directors, publishers
and architects, wore serious glasses and lined jackets,
drank quantities of superior scotch at our teenage parties.
I steered clear for fear of looking stupid and watched
my friends and the assembled sharp dressers grapple
with his late night sermons. He was the last person
I thought would have depression. He found me
on Facebook and said to visit when I got to Vermont.
He thought I knew but I didn't, not until we met
in his sparse kitchen. We talked of his divorce,
how his dad died of cancer when we were at school,
nights carrying his bony body up the shaky stairs.

3. Mousey's Mansion

I barely noticed her at school: she was mousey.
I assumed she just toed the line. She didn't wear
the latest fads, swoon or suck up to the in-group.
She was into science, even joined an after-school club
that held competitions with experiments, awarding ribbons.
I pitied her boring life; didn't recognise it as contentment
or a god-given fascination with how the world works
while we complained, as we must, about the drudgery
of lessons and homework. My friends and I shook
our energy all over the place, took jobs we didn't like
in bars and offices, tried to fix our self-esteem
with parties and lovers, shipwrecked our weekends.
I once got invited to her big verandah'd place
in a hip part of town. I was ashamed as I quietly
struggled to recall my passions. I wish I'd had
a fascination with beetles, meteors or Romantic poets.

4. Destructo with Gymnastics Medal

I wasn't in her inner gang but now I suspect
there wasn't really one. I hung around with her
when we were newly teenagers, wagging last period,
making joke phone calls, trying smoking. Delirious
with risk, I watched her swear at teachers, wreck books
and nick stuff from the corner shop as I sniggered
a few steps behind. I ran into her after she got expelled
and she told me to sneak out our windows late at night
to meet two older boys with a bottle of vodka. In the dark,
I felt so shaky, I slunk off home. When she proudly told
of what happened after I left, I got scared and avoided her.
One of the last times I saw her, she turned up at mine,
trolleyed, saying she smashed her mum's car (at fourteen!).
I closed the door on her as she yelled: *you're so lame!*
I was convinced she'd be dead or in jail before long
but recently I saw her photo, proud and middle-aged
with her pigtailed daughter holding a gymnastics medal.

5. Four Minus One Makes Zero

One of our inseparable Gang of Four, she had
something: a wide smile, a cute look, a spark
that attracted even the cool guys from other schools.
She got invited to the in-parties, picked up in cars –
left us for dead. We wrote her a shaky letter,
saying: *We know we're just dickheads...*, hoping
she'd say *No, you're not*, but she just rolled her eyes
and told us to grow up. At Uni, when you'd think
things would even out, we were at the bar
with her latest beau, talking about school days
and I told a story about her high school boyfriend
who ended up in jail. It was true, but that's when
she decided we weren't friends. I should have
apologised but I couldn't. I wanted to be seen.
I wanted her to say: *No you're not a dickhead.*

6. Born With It

People often say young children have a purity
but she had it like a glow. She stitched and decorated
little beds, curtains and rugs in her elaborate dolls' house.
She'd make us all milkshakes with a melting smile
when her mum came home from work too exhausted.
At that age, intention isn't complicated: everyone
is kind and you can make them happy. At high school,
she joined Greenpeace and the refugee support group,
headed rallies and committees, developed a slight scowl.
She'd snap that I didn't care enough or help fundraise.
I couldn't put it into words but I recognised something
familiar in myself in how she'd changed and it broke my heart.
I thought she'd rage against one cause or another all her life.
After she had three children of her own, she invited me
to volunteer at a homeless shelter. I was mesmerised,
watching her endlessly listening with her milky smile,
folding donated clothes. The glow had won out,
curled up the corners of her mouth, softened her eyes.

7. No-Shake Mohawk

His red-tipped mohawk appeared
quietly at school one day – it was
as if he was wearing a swear word.
We were impressed with the casual
shock of it. It improved his sneer,
which was sort of gentle. Otherwise,
he carried on with drinking and parties
like other boys in ripped jeans and
splatter T-shirts, but was pretty calm,
even when he passed out. When I
found out he'd become a crisis manager
for ExxonMobil it made sense for
someone who wore a mohawk like that.

8. Big Mouth Rises

I remember how sarcastic, but actually shaken up she was
reading her school report aloud. The form teacher wrote:
She'll only do something if she can make her own sense of it,
which she took as contrary, selfish, troublesome –
probably what was meant as our teachers were classic
at pretending to be positive when they wanted to
point the finger. She was always the one demanding
explanations for facts learnt by rote, wanting more time
to think which she did past the oval on the other side
of the bike shed, instead of maths. I can't remember why
I had a stand-up argument with her about one line in a book,
something about race and history. Her eyes were on fire;
it excited yet exhausted me. Her test marks were average
but it didn't bother her. A few years ago, I saw her
glammed up on TV accepting Journalist of the Year
and in the same argumentative way she had thanked
that teacher for his foresight, she raised that trophy up.

9. Middle-aged Karma

I was shaky drunk and weepy in a mauve ball gown
that fell awkwardly on angular bones. He sat
next to me and asked what was wrong as if he might
get a comprehensible answer when everyone else
had lost patience. With a square haircut, a 50-year-old
in 17-year-old skin, he didn't seem to want anything.
I wanted a ratbag with more attitude than I could muster,
someone to take me away, someone as cracked as I was.
Oh, I crashed and burned with the wrong ones for years
and decades later wondered what he was really like.
It seemed karmic that in our school reunion photo
he was the middle-aged spunk, shining in grey hair.

10. The Rickety Chair Guy

He was always around, connected to friends
of friends: that's how parties worked back then.
Too often, I'd end up stuck next to him
on a squashed-up sofa or cluttered pub table,
no matter how strategically I tried to arrange myself.
He'd say something sarcastic about everything:
he knew it all. It wore me down. I gave up
and went silent. He didn't even get it. Thank God,
I lost track of him for years, until one summer night
a bunch of us went to a party which turned out
to be his. His partner was a violinist with blue hair
who'd fallen in love with his manly jawbones.
At 2 am, I wandered into the garage for a break
and in the gloom he shoved a rickety chair under me;
we talked and he listened, the legs of the chair shaking.
Something had loosened in him and it was exhilarating.

11. Wild Skateboard Hero

It was all shaking: he'd never known anything else.
Small windows of stillness were too banked with emotion
and best kept on the hop with blots of cheap cider,
fat joints and random rages. Rather than get too close
I'd walk to the wrong bus stop and gaze at the distance.
I was slight and common enough not to bother with.
He thought the system deserved as much swearing
as he could muster and he was a wild skateboarder –
landed on his head enough times, often broke bones,
always covered in bruises to show he could risk flying
into concrete. He came to school jiggly and smarmy
the day after they found him comatose on the sports oval.
He had more indestructible lives than all of us put together
until he disappeared. The community paper reported:
Milk truck runs over local boy two blocks from school.

12. Kids but no DJ

I suppose us girls thought marriage was the thing –
underneath it all we were desperate to be promised
forever love and then we could get on with our life.
When she fell in love at fifteen her life seemed charmed.
They were the top school couple: beaming and entwined.
I never thought they'd ever break up, but one summer,
after we left school, he took off to Germany to DJ in a club
and never returned. I thought she'd be utterly shattered
but she got new tight dresses and a pale boyfriend
and just carried on. He was a wreck and year after year
she didn't seem to care: marriage in a crappy registry office,
pathetic flat, one baby, two more, his constant unemployment,
short on rent, her tiring two jobs. Out of the blue, she told me
she wanted kids at twenty and the DJ didn't but she loved
his electro-funk album. We put it on and shook all over.

13. Sturdy-framed Life

She was careful, covering up homework, hogging
novels and notebooks, always pulling up her clothes,
one hand over her breasts and never showing her legs
but her mouth was wide and wonderful and the boys
dropped like flies beside her as she picked over them
laughing, embarrassed, shy. I can't believe I never
asked her where she was before she arrived suddenly
at our school. She was too smart to worry about
and our three-hour phone marathons covered everything:
cliques, teachers, the whole damn complicated world.
I loved her sprawling questions and thought she'd be
a journalist or novelist but she always hid before
she could really shine and I felt powerless as she built
a plodding sturdy-framed life. At middle-age,
when many of our friends' flared dreams had fizzed,
she joyfully renovated her kitchen. I admired her contentment,
more so, when she told of those shaky years before we met.

14. Avoiding PE

I shuffle from lesson to lesson, weighed down
with judgement, avoiding PE and leotards at all costs.
I have no clue how to make myself into someone.
We discover sneaking out in the quiet of night –
no rules, no timetables – to meet boys, guzzle cider,
pass fags, nick street signs and chocolate bars,
climb over shaky fences marked 'No Entry'.
One night, two of us sleep in a building site
and after the joy of swiping a just-delivered milk bottle,
we tear down the street, climb a treehouse
and scream at the sunrise *Just watch us, world!*

2

The Glasshouse

The Clockhouse

The Glasshouse

the metta bhavana

In the glasshouse at the back of the garden,
we sit on frayed cane chairs amongst stacked pots,
unpeeled garden gloves, spilling packets of seeds:
someone I hardly know, someone I dearly love,
someone I don't really like who asks constant questions.

We're undisturbed in the cooling dip of night
with nowhere we have to be, just tinkering sounds
as we pour and cup light, sweet tea. There is steam.
One passes cherry chocolate; another slices pears
and peaches on a plate; a third offers lozenges.

The rusty lamp glows as we keep telling tales
you might at that hour, held in the mist
of the cracked windows disappearing into grass.
The night is a slow wonky-wheeled trolley.
Spiders carry on spinning as if we're incidental.

In the faint grey of early morning, we wander
into the garden then up into the body of the house –
an ordinary world where the day has not yet happened.
An upturned chair is balancing on its elbows.
Tools, dishes, papers are scattered like old bones.

But there's a warmth in our fingertips so strong
perhaps it can be sensed by others seeking warmth,
others who might sit in gardens through the night.
There's no distance between us, just this house
and the sprawling garden emerging into bright light.

A Respectable Life

It's not easy these days in a fully functioning modern flat.
Back when we were students, there was a crumbling hole
right through the lounge room wall into the kitchen where
random notes were left from a mysterious guy called Alan,
a sensitive serial apologist with an intense anger problem.

It's not easy in the quiet: just me, the radio, the clock.
No Vince with his excessive coat-tails, pockets of poetry
and noisy Ramones obsession, or Rach with her husky howl
and strapped-on beaten-up guitar, or Joe's gravelly ramble
telling bogus stories on late night talk-back radio.

No Brownlow brothers with a philosophical dilemma
and a pile of tinnies appearing in the lounge, or Lizzie's ex,
who was never really her ex, face pressed to her window
singing vodka versions of Eternal Flame at three in the morning.
It's not easy always being able to buy what you need

without interruption or subterfuge, days flowing like milk.
No anticipation of the end-of-week market specials stew,
Vince in Rach's polka dot bikini stirring, while she arranges
the bottle top collection blu-tacked to the wall and muses on
which hangovers are at The Pig & Hound sharing special chips.

Rolodex

It's as it was back then: still looking like a student house, full of peeling character and scrappy furniture. Inside the room I used as my office, there are now three desks, three offices. Space in this area is much more of a premium these days. A man sits at one of the old-style dark jarrah desks piled high with papers – the other two occupants are absent. Probably people work here part-time, odd days, on niche arts, campaigning or community projects, like I used to. I tell the man I once lived and worked here when it was a shared house. He makes small talk then says how he gave a threepence to a persistent ghost which seemed to settle it down. It wasn't a ghost I remembered but I couldn't help but wonder.

On another desk is a rolodex like the one my parents used to keep next to the rotary dial landline. At the top of where it's open is my name and number in thick marker pen and capital letters. There are other names printed underneath but in normal pen or pencil and not in capitals. I ask whose desk it is, but it's not a name I know. I must be significant. Perhaps we haven't spoken for years and she's been meaning to call when something falls into place? Maybe I've become a sort of aspiration? Do I have a crucial answer? Or perhaps she's confused me with someone else and heard I can do something that I can't. Or, maybe, I've done something she wants to complain about but she's not yet had the courage or enough evidence to make the call.

I thank the man for showing me around without mentioning my full name. I comment on the persimmon tree and woolly bush still going strong. It is a work of love here, he says. Of course, I say, without needing any details, I totally understand.

Party Invitations

You throw about party invites like confetti to friends and acquaintances, including people you hardly know. The risk seems reasonable. People like parties so surely many will come, even if they're not as fond of you as you might think. You're upbeat, easy-going but counting the invites like coins.

Unfortunately, on the night, most people have better things to do. Among the dozen or so who arrive by peak party hour, three are hard core friends, two neighbours and four were invited to make up the numbers, which would be okay if there were numbers but there aren't. More unfortunately, three people who you've always wanted at one of your parties suddenly arrive, well-dressed and expecting a party.

Meanwhile, a couple are in the kitchen, one person in the loo, two are making calls outside so that doesn't leave nearly enough for a party in the main party room. There isn't even much talk, let alone the crowd buzz you were expecting. You can't leave the room, so you do some careless dancing which doesn't fool anyone. The three desirable people huddle and when you turn around they're gone. You wonder how this will affect your social standing. One of the four invited to make up the numbers leads a surprisingly satisfying sing-a-long to *Hey Jude*. But on balance, it's probably best the other three left at this point.

Mr Jacob Never Seemed to Have Much Backbone

He never stood for much. Never sponsored
a student on a walk-a-thon. Nothing
stirred him. If you asked him a question,
he wouldn't give a straight answer.

He'd blubber something so we had no idea
what he meant. We wondered how his maths students
would have coped if it wasn't for text books.
No one knew how long he'd been around:

his suit the colour of the soupy carpet.
At staff meetings, he'd look gluggy, his face
translucent, eyes submerged. You wouldn't hear
his rubbery limbs when he came up behind you:

his weightlessness, his tap on the shoulder
like a surprising sponge. His office grew dank
with over-watered plants, five water jugs –
it wasn't a casual interest in the fish tank.

Miss Green caught him trying to climb into it,
one arm submerged, face dripping. His giddy stare
frightened the English teachers while science teachers
explained: *Rocks, pinned insects, test tubes,*

we all have our obsessions. This was different.
And it was a mistake to send Mr Jacob
on the year 9 seaside trip. He just gazed
at the sea. He was useless with the students,

then halfway through the beach cricket game
a kid threw seaweed at him. He seemed to like it,
took it in both hands, stood up, walked
like a man in a trance into the water.

Miss Green called out to him to no avail.
He never came up for air. No one went after him.
They didn't find a body, just a huge jellyfish
washed up in the bay and his useless glasses.

Our Front Garden

Every week she stands in our front garden
for at least a few minutes. Her gaze is clouded
but focused: there's nothing disingenuous about it.

She dresses up: shined shoes, lipstick,
a silver brooch clipping together a coat or shawl.
At first we thought she wanted something.

My husband spoke to her several times,
my daughter offered her cake – she didn't
take any notice. We left out a comfortable chair

but she preferred to stand. In the five years
we've been in this house, we've put up a fence,
had a paint job, pulled up the rose garden,

my husband's new truck pitched on the verge,
a tricycle bogged in the herb patch, but nothing
fazed her. We noticed that her red coat

was getting worn then she bought a blue one
with a black collar and matching gloves. Perhaps
coming here was the first time she wore them?

Her gentle humming is a good companion
to my husband's gardening. We look forward
to seeing her, watching her face change

as she steps off the kerb into our garden.
It marks our week. She's been late by a day or two
only a few times – I suspect for good reason.

Out shopping on the high road, I've seen her
on her way to our place and I admit following her
more than once – at a respectful distance.

There's a satisfying labour in her steps
up the steep pavement, across the muddy park.
Strolling behind, I feel a purpose in life

and a little envious. Caught in the traction of my week,
she seems to silence me with her presence so that
I wonder if I've lost my way, should be more

committed to something or dress better.
I'd like to send her a Christmas card,
but I think it's not appropriate. And if one day

she doesn't come, we wouldn't know what to do,
who to tell, how to mark it and our garden
would once again be like anyone's garden.

Taking Care of Clothes

I wouldn't say there was anything unusual
in donating large bags of clothes to a charity shop.
Several in a row would indicate a clear-out
but every couple of weeks I'd see her drop off a bag,

looking as if she should've kept some of it for herself
in her flowery jumper and tie-dye trousers.
And I wasn't judging her when I saw her across the road
standing on a step ladder peering into a skip,

hauling out clothes with a long-handled pick-up, dangling
one piece at a time like a questionable piece of meat.
Practised and professional, she'd examine it
with calibrated eye and nose, pulling it closer

in increments, before hurling it skilfully to the back
if it had irreconcilable rips or unimaginable smears of goop.
If a piece met approval, she'd drop it in a bin bag
tied to her workman's belt with a satisfied nod.

Just before my bus arrived, a jacket was hoisted,
dusty but unharmed and I wanted to say, 'I'll have that!'
She must have seen my eyes widen and fix so she called out
Find of the month! as if she'd panned a gold nugget.

Yep, Chanel, chain trim intact, one button missing, clean:
forty quid at least! Then I remembered it's a skip with dog poop
and garden muck and I was grateful my bus arrived.
So, wouldn't you tell the charity shop next time you passed?

They're our best sellers, Susi said, *washed in teatree, mended, ironed.*
So far, 48 bags and we're planning a party with cake for the 50th.
It's a movement apparently — four or five like her in our borough,
over a hundred in London — with clubs and competitive targets.

Bag for Life

It started with the Bag for Life
which no one took seriously despite
its name being blindingly obvious.
So, the Bags were microchipped

and if they were found junked
fines were issued. Not long after,
all garbage collections were cancelled –
so it wasn't just about the Bags.

No one wanted a house crammed with
old sponges, crisp packets, broken toasters,
disposable razors. Buying things became
serious research. It was no longer

casual, no longer a pastime, no longer
how we calculated national happiness
or personal status. Lifetime guarantees
were read properly. Things were made

biodegradable we never thought
possible. Tech upgrades meant simply
inserting microchips. Multiple-use
and re-use were big business. Inevitably,

composting was a growth profession.
Alongside council tax and water rates,
our household budgets included
personal waste management fees.

A certain inconvenience was
taken for granted. Borrow banks
flourished and people relied on
each other much more. I remember

as a kid at the supermarket, my mum
declined a Bag for Life, telling me we
didn't need it, it wouldn't make a difference.
Next, they're going to introduce inheritance.

Considered Questions

After a viewing of the work of black artists there is a Q&A session. The gallery manager kicks off and asks how their identity influences their art. We find out the artists are from very different countries. When the questions are open to the audience there is fidgeting, then someone asks how Hip Hop informs their work. But none of the artists have much interest in Hip Hop. Another asks if modern African art is having a resurgence – one of the artists mentions an African artist they admire that no one else has heard of and another artist notes how African masks influenced Picasso. A third audience member asks them about the influence on their work from protest movements such as Martin Luther King, whom the audience member greatly admires. The artist on the end of the panel says he died twenty years after she was born in Surrey. A second artist says Martin Luther King was a great man but he's more likely to be influenced by painters such as Chris Ofili. There is much nodding.

A Man My Father Played Golf With

And the previous weekend, as it happens, Mr Harris
played golf with my father in puff-ball plaids, his podge
of feet stuffed in fringed golf shoes, his face a basketball
caught in an exhaust pipe about to burst. His huge thunk
of a head could take up a whole mantelpiece where perhaps
it could rest now he's gone so we could gaze at his huge bones.
Mr Richard Harris owned his weight and weight mattered:
he measured his sway that way. If he fell, he could take out
everything underneath. The grass paled as he yelled at it
for the stupid government, stupid human rights morons,
idiot environmentalists. He missed an easy putt on the 17th,
thwacked his club and sent earth flying, then he and my father
discussed tactics of the game, the balls, the angle of wind
and banking cloud right up to closing time at the clubhouse.

The Circle Line

He says he saw me first at Kings Cross dashing
down the stairs, straight onto the train, loosening
my purple scarf, my chequered overcoat, panting
with relief, but I say it was Moorgate, when I noticed

his long black coat with its upturned collar appear
in my carriage as he intently studied a tube map,
pretending not to notice much else, as you do,
and although he says it had nothing to do with

the crowd thinning out at Monument, I'm sure
that's when he started to look up that bit longer,
loosening his lips as he saw me glance back,
incidentally, he said I sideways-smiled at him

at Cannon Street, but I must have been daydreaming
since I don't remember that particular stop at all
and it wasn't until Mansion House that I realised
his gaze had an intensity the exhausted tube crowd

didn't have as he picked up his paper, pretended
to read, then put it across his knee and sneaked
a look at me after a long intake of breath, repeating
this several times, and I also took out my book

and did the same, then at Temple our eyes coincided
and we stared at each other, my pulse ticking,
and at Embankment he daringly asked me:
What are you reading? when he could see

the cover from there and I answered just the title
of the book as though I was giving him my full name
and number; he pressed his mouth shyly as if
I'd told him much more and I think he suspected

I'd planned to get off at Westminster or maybe
St James Park and walk back but I felt heavy in my seat
and stayed and when he stood up at Victoria, an obvious
place to change, I shifted uneasily on my seat,

but he was only stretching his legs, then lost his seat,
moved one closer, asked: *Is it a good book?* then
opened his paper, I opened my book, he uncrossed
and crossed his legs, several times, as did I,

then at High Street Kensington I rummaged my bag
for a tissue I didn't really need and started to muse
on why anyone would take the Circle Line all the way
round rather than cut through on the Central Line,

and at Paddington, I wondered if anyone would notice
if I passed the stop where I got on as I watched him
diligently clock each station as we went by,
shuffling nervously, but at Baker Street, he sighed,

nodded, held my gaze with lowered eyes for at least
two full seconds as if to acknowledge that a chance
to make a dash south on the Bakerloo or Jubilee Line
and beyond was completely, expertly ignored

and I nodded back, pleased, as Baker Street felt like
an important mark of commitment and as we kept
circling, each time we pulled into Baker Street
there was a half-smile or a raised eyebrow,

but neither of us was sure where the beginning or end was –
after several Baker Streets we exchanged a bold sentence
or two and it felt almost disappointing and inevitable
that at some point we would have to disembark, somehow.

The Lady of the Basement

There's a slither of light from a mostly bricked-up window
in the basement under the post office where she can see
ankles, trolley and pram wheels, dogs' noses: all soundless.
One chair. One table. Exposed light globe. Ten packs of cards.

Time is muted down there with no sharp edges
of expectation or failure as she plays variations of solitaire.
Hours of it – slender moments of pleasure in making
order from no order. There. There. There. And turn over.

Each game takes as long as it takes without consequence.
Pleasure is simply given and not asked for. She yearns
for the contentment in laying hearts on hearts, ace to king,
absorbed in complicated strategies, tallies and pack switches,

the cards are a weight she leans into with their simplicity
of cause and effect and the effortless honesty of chance.
The end doesn't come easily, there's always a pulling back:
one more game, or two, or five – she loses count.

Night might descend. When the familiar present finally
pours back into her body it fills her with muddy sorrow.
She sits still, adjusting, and often picks up the cards again
for another round or so until the street empties above.

There's talk in the church, the houses and streets
of disappearances. Her phone is off and she never
says where she's been. 'She stays late into the night,
bless her, with a sick aunt.' 'She visits her son in prison…

it was self defence.' 'Does the archives for MI5.'
She walks the streets with stones in her shoes to the basement,
taking the fire escape stairs. Who would think to get down
on the pavement and look through that slit of window?

3

Far From Home

The Queensland Box Tree

This is my world, where I let my sandals drop
onto the grass below amongst the swaying pussy-tails,
the dandelions looking up at me like sun-winks.

This sweep of lawn, this forested garden in front of me,
the hedge leading to the letterbox, this house,
the street, these lowlands – this is my kingdom.

As I climb higher, the road trails off the edge
of my world: rooftops, tiny people carrying bags.
The top branch bows under my weight,

but it knows me well enough to hold.
The creamy flowers around me smell as sweet
as oranges and peaches. I balance on one foot

and when I slip, I catch with both arms –
hug a wooden limb, press it against my cheek.
Arms and legs scratched and alive, mouth full of spittle.

My magnetic sun, my vastness, my burning days,
my place etched on the landscape, rooted
and always lifting, lifting, holding.

House of Bricks

They say a house of bricks can stand up to a wolf
with breath like a hurricane. My dad grew up
in the Depression: he knows. In our house of bricks,

there was no Depression, but I dreamt of a hurricane
that levelled our house. I could see the wolf panting
next to the rubble, very pleased with itself

while we huddled in torn pyjamas; my sister
cradled her doll that had lost a leg and whispered
'don't worry', over and over into its plastic ears.

My parents pretended to make soup in the ruins.
When I woke up I went round the house pressing
walls and floors, the heavy dining table,

but when I sat in the big chair in the lounge
I could hear the wind howling down the chimney –
the beast warning us. My parents made a hearty roast

in our house of bricks and that's what counted.
Never speaking about the child who died
would not matter in a house as strong as this.

The Before

Inside a jarrah box carved with roses is warm air
from the day I met him in 1925 at Matilda Bay
when the flare of early summer drifted
up my skirt and inside the folds of my blouse.

He took my hand to ease my step from the jetty
to the swaying boat – goose pimples trickled
along my arms. Our eyes met then flicked away;
my hem brushed the damp deck but quickly

dried out and bright light spilled everywhere.
Granddaughter, there's a spot on the bow for you
with the breeze in your hair – hold on
as we skim the water together, face in full sun.

This is when we had everything at once –
it would have suited you, as much as it did me.
Here, I've kept the box for you, dug it out
from under the furs and beads. Inside

is the before: before the shrapnel ate him away,
before the wild temper and all that came after
and because of, all that meant we could not
reach you. Here, open the box, it's yours.

The Clock in Aunt Anna's Lounge

It suited the Victorian dark wood décor.
You called it tasteful. You said it was welded
into the wall, and if you wanted to remove it

you would have to take out the entire wall
and it was a structural wall in your mother's
mother's house so no one was taking out that wall,

plus it divided the kitchen and lounge which
needed to be separated. Its modest tick
could slip into the background but it also spoke

the unsaid things briefly and plainly when
least expected, things we barely dared to think.
Once when my mother was sipping tea,

it blurted out exactly what happened in that house
thirty-three years ago, then struck a clanging
twelve o'clock while you both sat stunned.

My mother didn't visit again for months.
That caterwauling clock woke you in the night.
It got to you like a wounded child, a jilted lover,

a smart aleck, a confidant. I saw you hold
its filigree frame and whisper 'centuries of wood
are breathing', its blue steel hands, rigid.

You abandoned yourself to openness,
listened more than anyone could, though
its constant tick left you thin and bereft.

It knew your private ghosts by name, told you
the creak on the back steps was what you thought
and time and space were thinner than suspected.

The horologist who serviced it would eye you,
saying 'You'd better look after this gem.' It purred
with smugness when he turned his back.

I may have heard that clock murmur once or twice
but it never spoke directly to me. I was twelve
when you were gone. Standing in front of that clock,

sun squeezing through the blinds, sparks of gold
flickering from its pendulum, I started to cry
with the one o'clock metal on metal chime,

the fading ring of springs. I didn't want it to see me
like this but I wish I could tell you that we're
more adrift, we miss you and I believe you, all of it.

There are Places to Remember Sadness

Some days, the shops are shut, the traffic lights
pause; our faces drop, our hands fall empty.

Some days, we watch and listen to the rain
from towers, custom-built, all glass and tin.

Some days we do not speak. Some days we just
sit side by side. Some days we don't wear shoes.

Great Uncle

How I wish for an uncle, a tough talkin' bloke,
Who'd be rough as his bush-hat, and wiser than most.
He'd be churlish and hard, but he'd whisper to me:
You're a gal with an eye that's much finer, you'll see.
          And he'd tease me and tell me to
          Never take things,
     Never take things as they come.

How I wish for an uncle who'd stride into town
With his confident grin that's so widely renowned.
He'd be smellin' of ash in his rabbit skin hat,
Gettin' lattes for free, charming waiters with chat.
          And he'd cheer me and tell me to
          Never take things,
     Never take things as they come.

How I wish for an uncle who cuts all the crap.
He'd be mates with the mayor and invite the shy tramp
For a candlelit dinner while jamming some funk,
Then he'd make the best stew and inventions from junk.
          And he'd soften and say to me
          Never take things,
     Never take things as they come.

How I wish for an uncle whose shack is one room
In the deep of the wood, in the crack of the moon.
He'd know all the names of the plants and the stars
And he'd teach me when I was alone in the dark.
          And he'd goad me and tell me to
          Never take things,
     Never take things as they come.

The Drake

Now that I think about it, there was always a swampy smell.
Often a smudge of mud across the kitchen tiles:
I'd examine the shoe rack but all the soles were clean.
I thought all backyards had leaves, twigs, gumnuts, snails,

and many feathers even though we were miles from a lake.
A neighbour asked me once: 'Do you have a chicken?'
At times, I'd wake in the night to what sounded like a horn,
but then silence, no engine. These things happen in a city.

After the silence there was a scuttling that could've been
any wide flat feet slapping on concrete paving.
The first time I saw him it was an ordinary day:
he stood there in the yard on an upturned pot plant,

his blue-green-fawn sculpted feathers like a painting.
I carried on with my homework, didn't think that much of it.
I knew it was the same drake that turned up at school:
at first perched on the windowsill, preening, then

under the desk next to me, so when I went to read out
my project to the class, his honk made me stutter
and I slipped on his damp trail. In assembly they asked
who wanted to join the choir, but I didn't get up –

he was jammed between my ankles and I didn't want
to tread on his flippers or cause a stir from his shrieking.
He'd follow me home and it took me much longer to ride a bike
because of his flapping about. Maybe he did mean well

but I wished he wasn't there when I plucked up the courage
to talk to Sean Chambers. He kept ducking under my feet
so I walked funny and that day he smelt really badly of pond.
I kept my distance from Sean in case he thought the whiff was me.

At high school, I took up table tennis: it was good for balance,
timing and duck dodging. We even won a knock-out tournament,
the duck and I; despite his struts across the table,
his spluttering at the umpire. When I got the trophy home,

he watched as I inscribed 'The Drake' under my name in ballpoint.
I daydream of one day strolling past a lake when I'm old
and see him, looking me in the eye, standing just like he did
on that flowerpot with his perfect feathers, watching me go by.

It Didn't Happen Until University

I said I'd done everything else: just not that.
My room-mate, Sylvia, was astonished.
She lit a candle and said, *Tonight it'll burn down.*

I could already smell his turpentine skin,
hear his late night arguments on existentialism,
his heavy feet shuffle while I'd try to sleep.

I turned up late and unannounced. He smiled
like he knew everything. I never said I wanted love,
just to know what the thing was, to be one of those

who could be fresh-picked. He stroked the curve
of my lace vest, saying: *Very nice, very nice.*
He said he was falling in love with me, but I knew

he fell in love often. I was in love with longing
and thought only of flesh, leaving the rest behind.
It was a strange thing to be doing with two bodies,

especially in the awkward moments, the urgency
paused, legs stuck together, everything exposed,
the birthmark on my thigh lit red. Wrapped in a sheet,

hair dishevelled, I was surprised when I saw
my dewy face in the still white of the sink.
That was the best part: I remembered I was blessed

with the enamel skin of gods, perfect brown limbs.
Afterwards, we sat back to back as if we'd not yet
learnt to speak face to face. *Sex is sex*, he said,

as though I had simply joined the human race.
We argued. The tea was tepid. When I got home
Sylvia said, *I told you, I told you*, while I cried.

The River People

One day they just arrived, camped for days
on our river island, waiting for swans, but none came.
We don't know who they were, why they weren't
moved on. They were sun-blushed, ethereal,
used hand signals we'd never seen before.

On our daily commute across the highway
from island to city and back, we watched
their canvas tents and sometimes a figure or two
of a man, woman or child walking in the hot dust
like a mirage. The bridge's heavy traffic drowned

any sound of the birds, tides, their daily doings.
We couldn't tell them when the swans disappeared.
Would you have noticed if a highway, a skyscraper,
or if the river vanished and there was just gravel
under your feet? Will you still call this place

Swan River? We felt their heavy ochre eyes.
They made a swan shrine from a mass of grass,
bark and reeds: its beak pointing skyward,
long pampas grass feathers flying in the breeze.
Every time we crossed the bridge we felt the loss,

imagined their reflections in the water swimming
with glossy black swans. One day, the River People
just went. We didn't get to ask them anything.
The shrine eventually let go into the wind,
blowing into the river, into our Swan River.

Finding Australia

for Miss Brockman

We learned the directions of the compass, names of brave sailors
who sounded like philosophers, coloured in their sailing ships,
drew map after map that tracked noblemen spun by wild winds
who tried to find spices, and almost found Australia.

Unwieldy ships were washed up on far-flung reefs or islands.
When finally they found it, they put up flags on hilltops, nailed
plaques to trees. Captain Stirling was certain he'd found Perth,
so certain he brought boatloads of people down the Swan River

to witness it, commission paintings, build houses, forge roads.
Australia was young and proud, our future was on a plate.
We filled our project books with drawings of early settlers
in smart soldier outfits, women in long skirts and bonnets.

They kept on finding, as they trekked through rugged terrain
to discover more and more of what had not yet been found.
We coloured in more maps, listened to stories of hardship
when tattered men perished for us in search of an inland sea.

Then our eccentric year 9 social studies teacher whispered:
Terra nullius? Terra nullius? Australia was not discovered:
there were already people here right across the beaches,
plains, forests and deserts, who knew every bump and echo.

She showed us slides of black men in chain gangs, eyes disjointed
with shock, frightened black women in shift dresses, archives
of river poisonings and battles for land where only one side won.
She showed us modern photos of black people on reserves

with scattered rubbish and makeshift houses staring out of the dust,
told of a whole generation of children taken from their parents.
There weren't any pictures of brave men in sailing ships.
I wondered if we'd dreamt it all and what else they lied about.

The Story

No one spoke of what came before.
There were only two jokes.
His father crashed a car into a fish shop
on his way to go fishing at the pier.
His mother was in a beauty contest
because someone else was stuck in traffic.

And one thin story about how they met:
they took the same bus for two years.
In the back of his throat were questions.
Did his father get into trouble?
How did his mum do in that contest?
But there was always something to attend to

or the TV talking about how to cook a flan,
Egyptian art, whether there was life on Mars.
Out shopping, his mum said how a shirt collar
was like the one dad wore on their wedding day.
Was it a big wedding do? he asked, hoping
for a seed of story. *I'll buy in the sale,* she said.

His grandma was the only other one to ask,
but she backed out of story long ago.
When he finished school would he simply
bleed into adulthood like ink on blotting paper?
The TV flashed with war in Iraq, the legacy
of the potato famine, the fall of the Roman Empire.

Island Bay, New Zealand

I take the winding school bus to the cup of white beach
with rock pools that I'd been craving to see.

The closer I get to the water, the more I notice:
endless strains of seaweed: baubley, glassy,

fat and rubbery, with branches like tiny fallen trees,
and eccentric sponges, anemones, pink translucent

and murky brown jellyfish with clots of tentacles;
I pick up shells, shells, shells... starfish. I fantasize

I'm the first to discover this place, facing into the gale,
alone in the wild, gliding with the terns,

yet there's an ache that's not just homesickness.
I remember that in my beach back home

there *were* spidery black and blood-orange starfish,
red-legged hermit crabs and many more sea-jewels

in fizzing sand and rock I can't quite recall.
I didn't notice when they all went, quietly,

so quietly. The sand and shallows became barer
as the boats mowed the bay after the reefs

were blown up to let the big cruisers through.
I collapse on my knees into sand like I did

as a kid on my pink-and-yellow daisy bedspread
where I'd cry harder because I didn't understand why,

with all the noise, no one came. A fledgling seagull
swoops and catcalls before the wind sweeps it away.

Watermarks

Watermarks are etched on the back
        hands, across lined foreheads;
skin banks around knuckles and knees
        like waves breaking

a well-worn rhythm of muscle and bone
        swimming in the safety of fluid.
The loop and whorl of our fingertips
        leave tiny treadmarks

on all we touch, micro-ripples
        on bench tops, windowpanes,
banisters, fine tidelines threading
        across cups and coins

that pass between us. We're drawn
        to watery horizons, to shorelines
and follow chattering streams tugged
        into hushed, darker expanses.

We watch coils from raindrops spread
        across puddles and can almost hear
the hiss of sap drawn through the reach
        of tree trunks, stems, leaf tips

or seeds bursting with a drop of moisture.
        We place our hands
on our bodies and feel the longing, trace
        watermarks across our skin.

Rubber Dinghy with Glass-bottom Bucket, Rottnest

for Bob

Take your homemade glass-bottom bucket,
a certain uselessness, a disinterest in direction,

find a bay with patchwork reefs, far from people
and their things, wade into the cooling shallows,

lie across the rubber dinghy, tuck the oars away
and let the current drift you slowly out of your depth.

Hold the bucket steady in the water, let it draw you in —
before long you won't take your eyes off this porthole

into amniotic blue-green with its impossible detail.
The rubber is sun-warmed and fluid like water,

like the body as it softens into the tugging seabed;
the dinghy is a shadow on water, a cloud passing over.

All carries on underneath: wrasse jerk,
changing direction, a rush of whiting disperse,

then a hovercraft stingray! Ah seaweed sways
in slow motion, crab claws rise with a change of current,

a pale stone on the sandy bottom is a flounder gliding.
Look up from the bucket and it will only drag you back:

the sea's surface is too opaque to bear,
its blur of dark and light is the rim of a sky

you want to be under. After you're blown
into a cove, bumping on the sandy shallows,

minnows imagining they're sharks in deep water,
grains of sand running with the tide, a tumbling shell,

long after you're beached, as you stare
at the unfamiliar dry world, a transparent curtain

of currents, eyeing creatures, sea ribbons, reef,
coral will fall across your lids when you blink,

limbs streamlined, body held in tingling disbelief
that there's more than one world you can belong to

and how easy to slip between them, unmoor your mind
and live among the strange and shining.

Bunyip on the End of My Bed

When I go back to bed the umpteenth time,
he is there sitting on the end of my duvet,
his sprawling, nobbled feet squashed in the gap
between my bed and the wardrobe.

Getting back under the covers is awkward
with his bulge taking up so much room.
I curl up and settle as he speaks compulsively
as if drawing out a long thread coiled in his throat.

You know damselflies have thousands of lenses in each eye.
When a nymph crawls away from the water and first
breathes air, its skin splits open and two sets of wings rise up.
Yesterday, I saw three transformations in one hour –

he pauses, mostly for his own gasp and dreamy out-breath.
I don't interrupt even if he sounds off for an hour or so –
which isn't unknown – not just because I'm interested
but because nobody else talks to me like this any more.

There are interludes. He sees sweet wrappers
on my bedside table: *You ought to give that up –*
the plastic I mean, every year three hundred million tons
are thrown out and twenty million end up in waterways…

These facts he's recited many times and I don't mind –
I wish they were said more often elsewhere.
Once or twice he'll thwack a flipper on my duvet,
his cavernous nostrils swell, fanged teeth bare:

this time describing the Azure Damselfly
swooping on a midge with pinhead precision.
I'm very glad my bed has an iron frame
and I can see why some people think he breathes fire.

There are quieter moments when he turns to me,
though my head is heavy on the pillow with half-sleep
and whispers a little-known fact as if I might be
the only human to hear it, and maybe I am.

I try to hold those words but I forget them by morning.
Each time, he says he's glad we're friends then lopes off,
tripping over my boots, and even though we're both
a bit lost, I think it's better he's not bottling it all up.

Bunyip in the Kitchen

It's a surly dim night with street fights outside
but I know he's popped in as there're muddy drips
on the floorboards into the kitchen. Somehow
he's carried a bucket of shallow sandy water

with his clumsy flippers and lifted it to the table.
Drowsy and unimpressed, I re-tie my dressing gown.
Real water, he says, rapping his claws on the sink,
then scoops the water into a salad bowl with a tea cup

so I can see it better. Still, my pea eyes are no match
for his bulging globes with slit zoom lenses
so he gives me a hefty magnifying glass which
I curse, trying to focus – damn murky water at this hour –

but as I pull back I see a couple of water skaters then
get my eye into a world of flicks, hops, zips, whirrs,
of mites, beetles, springtails, worms, feathery unknowns
and I'm glued for some time, emerging to a snore

like a motorbike frog in a downpipe, and squished
in the dishwasher/washing machine corner,
his scaly beanbag-body is curled, webbed feet
turned up, ears shuddering like flags in a breeze.

It's lighter grey outside. I leave him there –
I can't disturb his contentment or risk
a wild roar if he jerks awake that could shake
the street with fright. He'll be gone by morning.

When the Insects Disappeared

In the centre of town at one of those
festivals with blasts of music and all
kinds of cuisine, fruits, sauces, spices
from all over the world, we ordered
and ordered, rustling packets, opening
and slicing, chewing and slurping,
laughing and chatting. The tables
were painted with spring flowers,
there were funky animal banners
from tigers to ibis, ten-foot batik giraffes
and a gently swaying digital wheat field
in the floor which had a calming effect.

We'd remarked how there were
no flies to bother us and much later
some of us noticed how quiet
the birds were. Weren't there more
sounds when we were younger?
The feasts continued, our days
circling as they always did, between
work and release. Later that summer,
food started disappearing in shops
and menus. The first few items
were seen as seasonal blips though
there were the usual complaints.

A certain silence had expanded
into the fields and forests – the air
was crisp, but the wind strangely lonely.
Complaints turned to anger when coffee
and chocolate became hard to find.
The Government was blamed. There was
much discussion on what insects
had to do with coffee and although
people understood more, it didn't change
anything. There was an eeriness that nobody
knew what to do with. There didn't
seem to be anyone answering back.

Jar, Grant Museum of Zoology, University College London

What we have here is a jar with folds
of striped fur, skin and innards
in pond-coloured formaldehyde.

Beside it is a photo of a man
dangling his trophy, its jaw loose,
the largest gape of any known mammal,

its tapered kangaroo-like tail limp
and trailing on the ground. This man
looks very pleased in his best jacket.

They called it tiger, wolf, hyaena, dog –
it's none of those – but a one-off marsupial
whose awkward gait meant it was easily

worn down. They thought these creatures
killed all the sheep, but now we're not
so sure and they didn't study the species

though they were on show in 13 zoos
including New York, London, Paris, Berlin,
various circuses and private menageries

and 2184 were bagged in those 21 years
the Government offered a tidy bounty.
Wilf Batty shot the last one in the wild

after it went for his chickens in 1930.
He sold it for a fiver, then it toured
Australia stuffed. Six years later,

the Government declared the animal
protected, the same year the last one
paced a concrete cage in Hobart Zoo

after it was left out in the cold. They still
mark the date: 7th of September 1936.
There're toys, trinkets, key rings, the usual.

The logo for the State Government,
for Cascade Premium Light Lager
and the Tassie cricket team, is a Thylacine.

Two hold up the Tasmanian coat of arms.
Scientists say the species can't be resurrected
from DNA fragments but there are

a few skeletons, desiccated body parts
and pickled specimens in museums
like this one. And in the next cabinet –

At Least

Senate re-vote Western Australia, April 2014

It's a rattling day in the crux of jet lag. I lose
       everything: leave my jacket on a park bench,
my bank card inside. When I go back, the jacket's
       empty. My friends try to help with tea and toast,
useful suggestions, but I've lost my phone somewhere
       between the park and their place, so I take the loop bus
round twice and don't find it. I feel weightless as if I'm still
       flying over the Middle East. My mind thins
after hours of confirming my identity on their house phone.
       I find my sunglasses in bed sheets but
the day's shot. Though I still have to vote – so my friends
       drive me to White Gum Valley Primary
where there are two charred sausages in the sausage sizzle,
       a huddle of well-dressed placard wavers,
no mid-afternoon queue. At the absentee desk,
       the woman asks me for ID. I feel so adrift
when I say: *I have none.* She asks me questions,
       looks me in the eye and somewhere between
her saying *It's OK* and handing me the ballots I feel
       my feet land, the smell of BBQ and sea air
hit like sheet iron and I'm almost about to cry. That night
       at Gino's, after an hour of pushing my empty cup,
my friend looks up from her phone, kicks me under the table:
       At least Scott Ludlam got a surge back into the Senate.
I land again: diesel, coffee, a woman shouting nearby.

If I Could Wake

If I could wake beside your warmth again,
this time in love with all your awkward pauses
as if we're driving slow on gravel in rain
and steering with care amid the flying stones;
if I could listen, not to my own reaching
but the heat inside our palms without the pride;
if I knew the wreck my heart was in could sting,
how much my flat replies could hurt, could hide,
I'd leave your terrible style, your stubborn ways
alone though overwhelmed and lie with you
entwined. Still, now I know how it all plays,
despite ourselves, how neat it seems, how plain,
if we're twenty, one more time, I'd leave again
the same, just more bewildered, more to lose.

The Phone is Ringing

for Suz

The phone is ringing under the floorboards
at 28 Edward Street which has been done up now
so there are no holes in the verandah floor.
The linen-suited tenants complain about the noise.

The phone is ringing inside a dark red rose
on Curlew Road, that smells unbelievably sweet
but they're all inside, partly deaf, doors closed,
the blue TV light flashing across the windows.

I hope the loud ringing is breaking the silence
of a maths class at Hollywood High, inside
Mr Hennessey's desk drawer. But it's all housing estate
now and the muffled ring is far underground.

The phone is ringing off the pier at Cottesloe,
near where a concrete paddling pool used to be.
It's cold and blustery and no one is going out
to the pier today with those thrashing waves.

The phone is ringing in the spider pot plant
where I put my stone collection you laughed at,
but you're not in the garden today, neither
is your neighbour, only your sleeping cat.

It's ringing at our Arc de Triomphe meeting spot
but it's drowned out by the traffic – so many people
but no one to answer it. Someone calls out
to the back of a head: *Is that you, I don't believe it?!*

The phone is ringing at Webster's corner shop
inside a stack of Canarvan bananas but the shopkeeper
ignores it, thinking it's kids messing about again.
There's no other reason that fruit would be ringing.

The phone is ringing in the next suburb from yours.
I misdialled. I was thinking of something else.
It's ringing in a flat where I had a boyfriend who kissed
in the doorway and promised a different life.

It's ringing on the verge of the house where you grew up,
though verges are big in this part of town.
It's ringing in your empty parents' kitchen:
the terrier twitches, the tabby cocks its head.

It's ringing at your place, by the computer and you
pick it up but you're not very interested to talk,
you haven't eaten much and can't taste. It's ringing
in your driveway and keeps ringing through the night,

it rings for weeks while you drive to your brother's,
your parents', feed the tabby and terrier, drive
to the funeral parlour and back again. The phone's ringing,
sweetheart, it's all I have this far from home.

Acknowledgements

Some of these poems were published in *Sleeping with Rivers*, which won a Seren/Mslexia pamphlet prize and was a Poetry Book Society Choice. Some were short-listed for the Manchester Poetry Prize in 2015. I acknowledge the following publications which previously published versions of these poems: *Rialto, Loose Muse Volume 1, Southbank Poetry, Quadrant, London Grip, In Protest:150 Poems for Human Rights* (The Human Rights Consortium, University of London). 'Dhanakosa, Scotland' was second in the Poetry School/Resurgence Poetry Prize in 2017, and 'How I Hold the World in This Climate Emergency' was Highly Commended in the same prize (now called The Ginkgo Prize) in 2019.

A huge thank you to the Arts Council England for support in completing this manuscript and to my wise and invaluable friend and mentor, Mimi Khalvati. This book wouldn't be half of what it is without Mimi's encouragement, guidance and kindness. Immense gratitude to Amy Wack and all at Seren Books for creating this book and having faith in me, and to Sadie Tierney for the gorgeous cover image. I'm grateful to the Katharine Susannah Prichard Writers' Centre in Perth for a residency in 2018 where some of these poems were honed.

Heartfelt gratitude to many poets who helped me along the way, including Malika Booker, Roger Robinson, Jacob Sam-La Rose, the Malika's Kitchen collective, Moniza Alvi, Roddy Lumsden, Pascale Petit, John Hegley, Saradha Soobrayen, Baden Prince Jnr, Kayo Chingonyi, Alison Winch and Peter Daniels. Kate Potts, Karen McCarthy Woolf, Jocelyn Page and Miriam Nash have also been invaluable in reading drafts, providing feedback or coming with me on inspiring writing trips. Also thanks to my feedback group members over many years (including Mona Arshi, Gale Burns, Pam Johnson, Rishi Dastidar, Edward Doegar, Selina Rodrigues, Denise Saul). Support from friends in England and Australia has been invaluable, including Gail, Kathy, Kath, Nic, Shona's gang, Eitan, Margo, Julie Watts and all the writers I've met in Perth. Many thanks for warm encouragement from Helen Mort and Philip Gross.

And to John for being the most supportive and loving partner in life I could ask for – and also pretty sharp at pointing out where a poem isn't working.

Poems written in first person that refer to family members don't necessarily reflect my real family members.